GRAPH GAMES

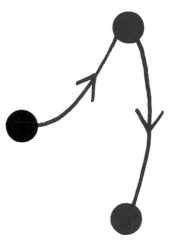

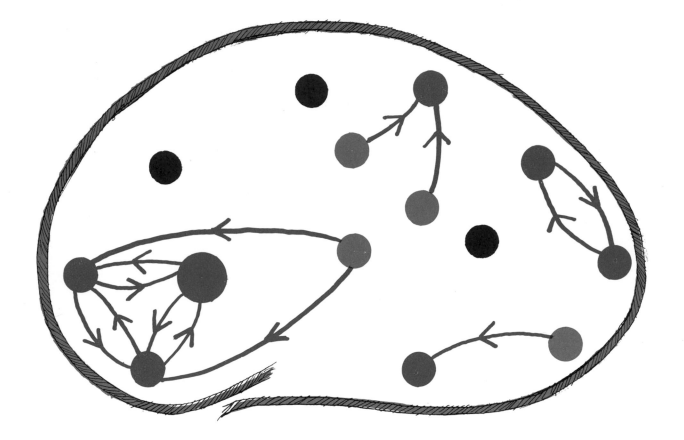

GRAPH GAMES

BY FRÉDÉRIQUE AND PAPY

ILLUSTRATED BY SUSAN HOLDING

1971

Thomas Y. Crowell Company   **New York**

YOUNG MATH BOOKS

Edited by Dr. Max Beberman, Director of the Committee on
School Mathematics Projects, University of Illinois

Edited by Dorothy Bloomfield, Mathematics Specialist,
Bank Street College of Education

VENN DIAGRAMS *by Robert Froman*

Copyright © 1971 by Georges and Frédérique Papy

Illustrations copyright © 1971 by Thomas Y. Crowell Company, Inc.

Manufactured in the United States of America

L.C. Card 72-157647
ISBN 0-690-34964-5
0-690-34965-3 (LB)

3   4   5   6   7   8   9   10

GRAPH GAMES

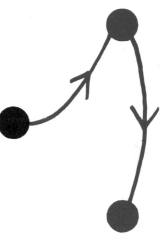

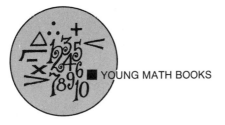 YOUNG MATH BOOKS

Here I am with my friends, playing in the yard be-
hind our apartment building.
You have probably guessed that I am the big dot.

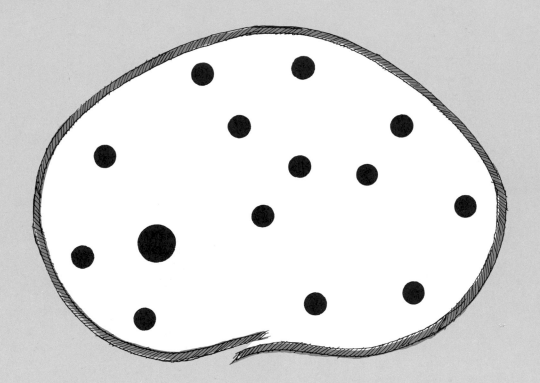

I have put a string around us to show that we form
a set.

No doubt you would like to see the boys and the girls. That is just too bad. They are all dots!

You don't even know whether I am

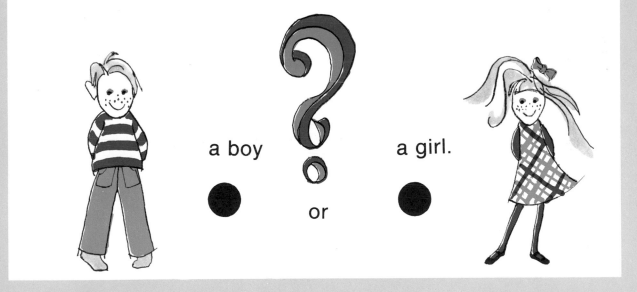

a boy or a girl.

We played "point-to-your-sisters."
Here is how it looked.

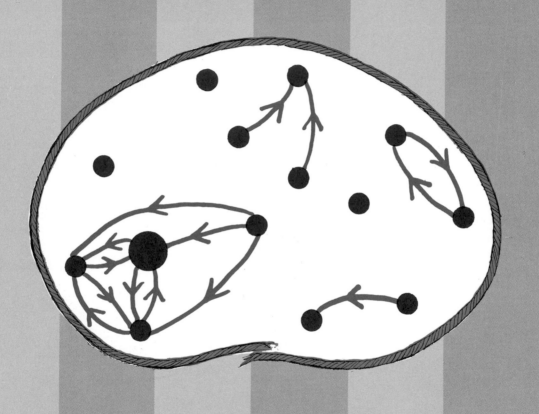

You can play, too, if you copy this graph onto a
piece of paper.
Use a red crayon to draw the arrows.

Now can you find some girls?
Color the girls in your drawing red.
And then turn the page.

All the children shown by red dots are girls

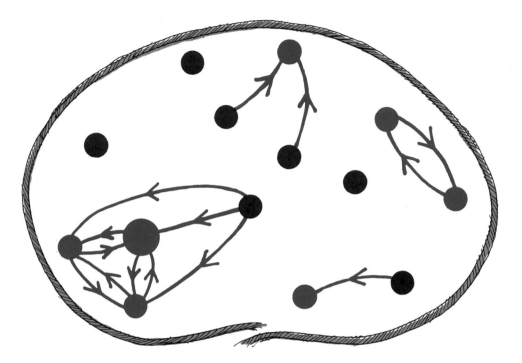

because every sister is a girl.

So you can see that I am a girl!
But perhaps you already guessed that because I
talk to you so sweetly.

My sisters Dorothy and Ann are playing with us.
    You can see where they are.
But you don't see my sister Irma. She is in Tim-
    buktu.
You also see my little brother John, who is point-
    ing to all three of us.

                                We aren't pointing to him.
                                He is not our sister!

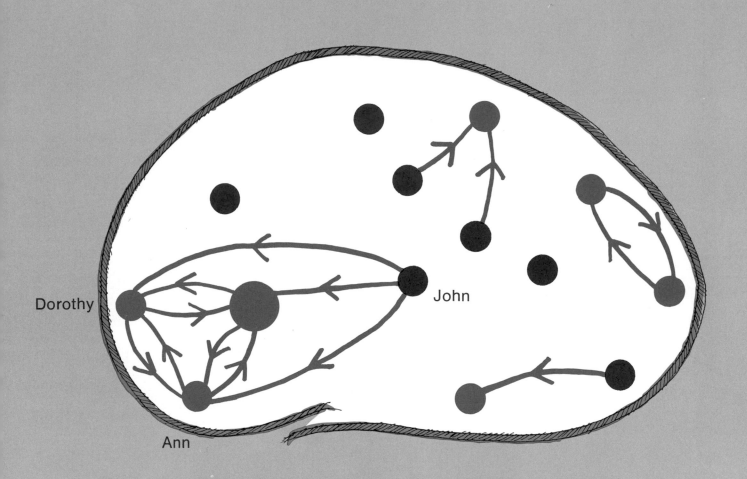

Dorothy

John

Ann

By playing "point-to-your-sisters," we found girls and also my sweet brother John.

By playing "point-to-your-sisters," we can find boys.

Color in blue all the boys you can find in your drawing.

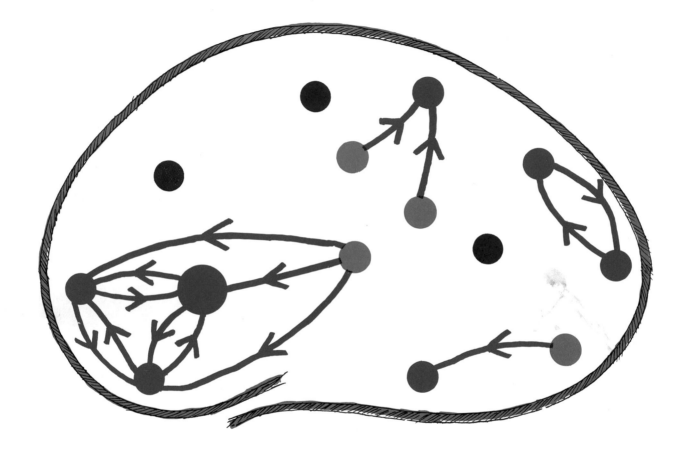

Instead of playing "point-to-your-sisters," we could
    have played "point-to-your-brothers" and
    drawn arrows in blue.

            Which blue arrows can
            you now draw for sure?

Draw as many as you can on your own picture.
And then turn the page.

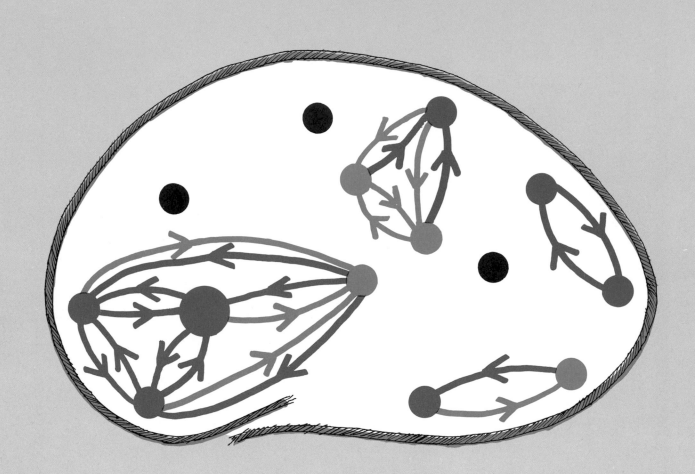

Compare your drawing with this one.

The children in the yard played
"point-to-your-brothers"

and drew all the blue arrows.

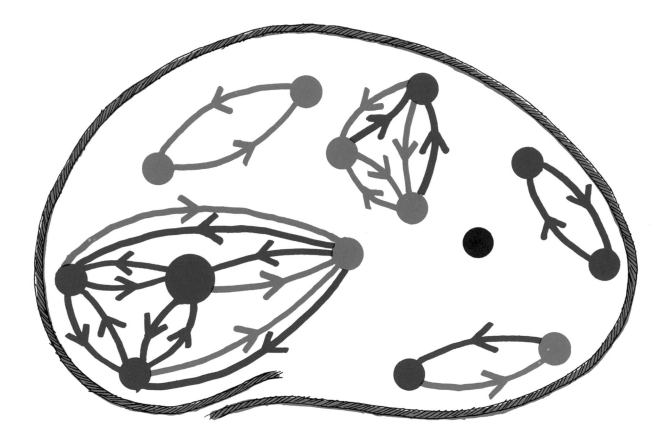

Compare your drawing with theirs.

Did you really draw all the blue
arrows you could find?

The children in the yard found some arrows
that you could not know about.

Ned and Ralph are brothers that the "point-to-your-
sisters" graph does not allow you to find.

BECAUSE THEY HAVE NO SISTERS HERE!

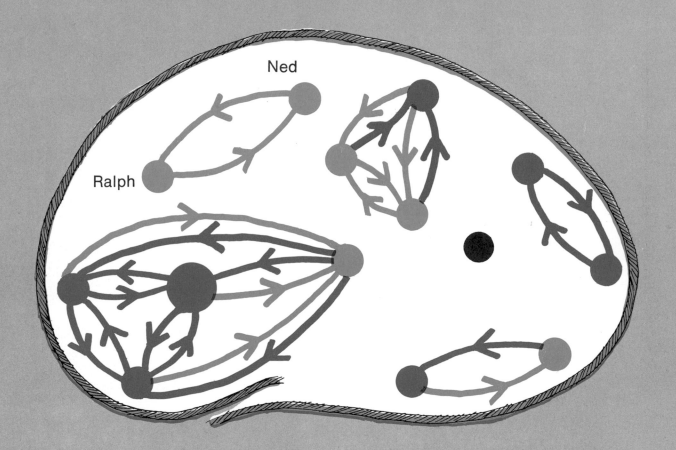

Ned

Ralph

It is perfectly possible for two boys
to have the same sister.

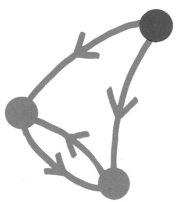

From the graph of the sisters, you
know that they are brothers!

The postman came into the yard.
He lives next door.
He knows all the children in the building.
Here are the letters he is going to deliver to the
children.

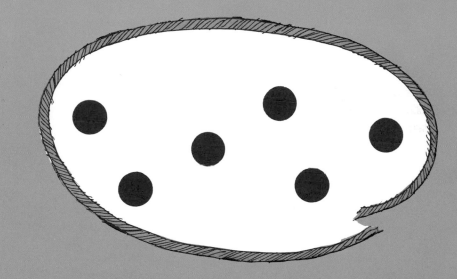

Who are the letters for?

Let us see who gets them!

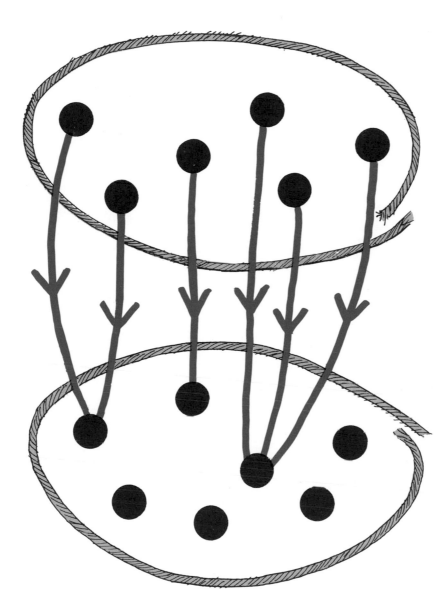

If you want to play this game, copy the drawing of
the letters and the children in the yard.
Point to the children who received one letter or
more.
Put a blue string around them to separate them
from the others in your drawing.

Can you find Charles?
Today is his birthday, and he got more letters than
anyone else.

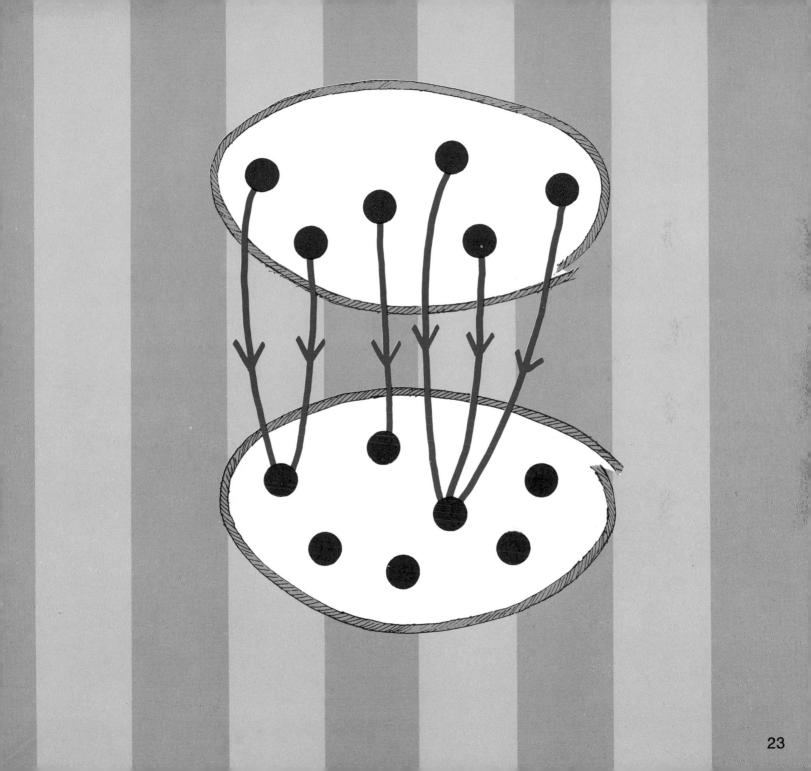

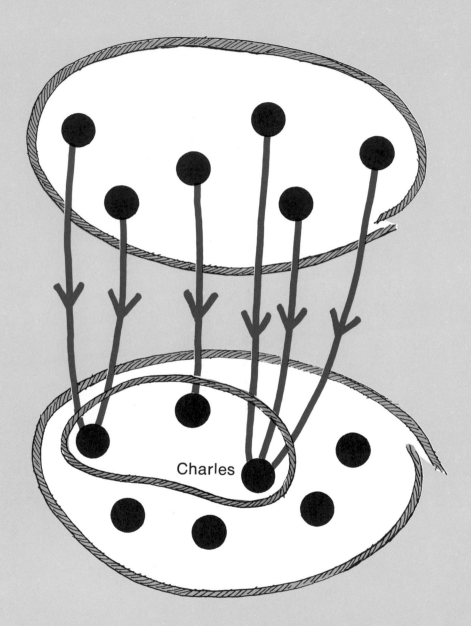

I am not inside the blue string.

But next week I will be.

It will be my birthday.

I think I'll get even more letters than Charles.

In your drawing, draw a blue string around the package of letters Charles received.
Do the same for the other two children.

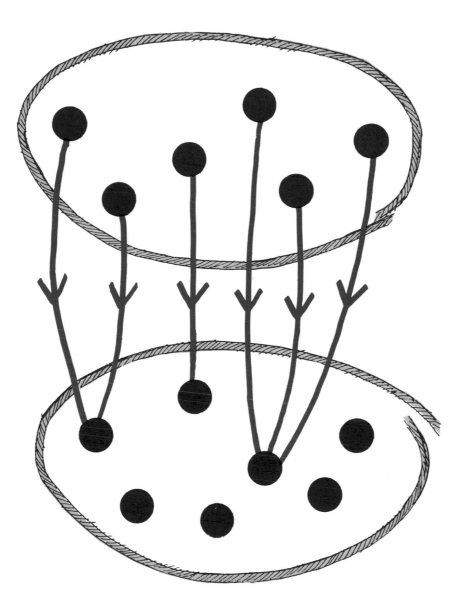

27

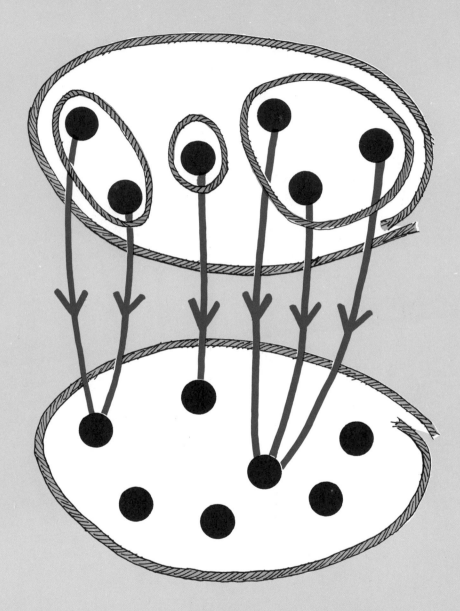

The girls are gossips.

They have told everyone about our game.

Some children are playing it in the schoolyard.

They are pointing to

    the sisters with red

    the brothers with blue

The bell rings before they finish their drawing.
Will you copy their drawing onto a piece of paper,
finish it for them, and at the same time color
the boys and girls?

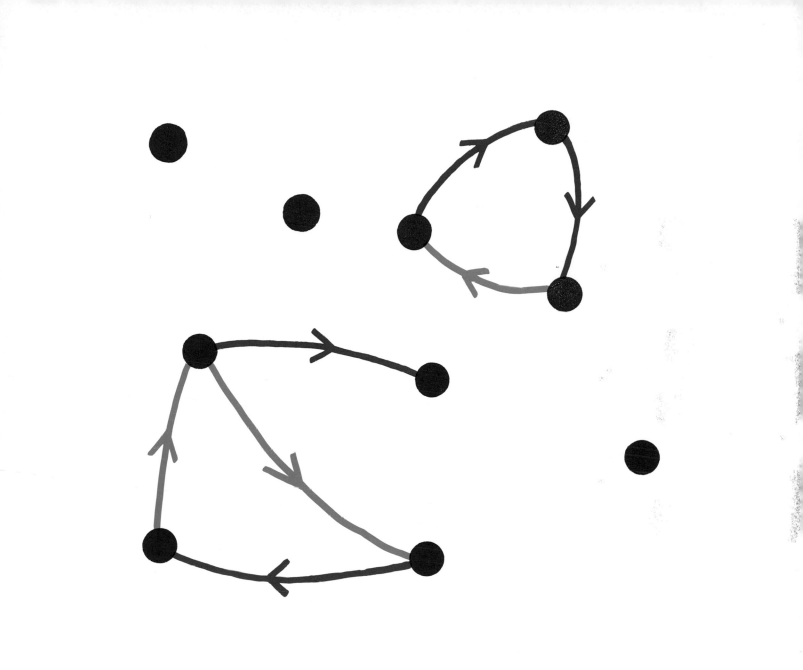

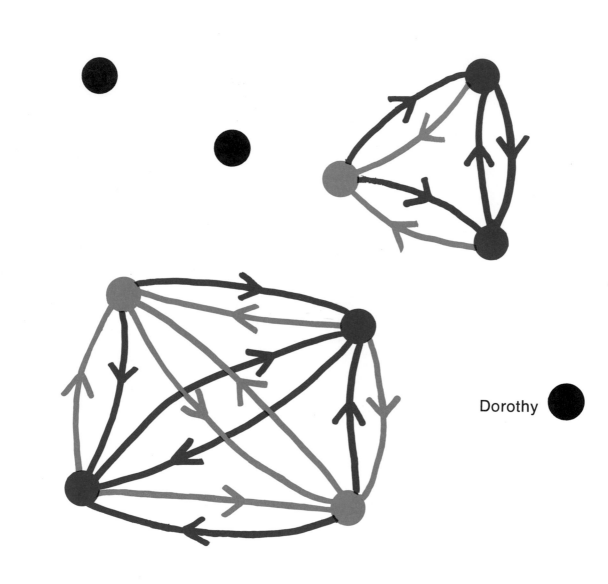

Dorothy

My sister Dorothy was playing with these children.
I wasn't there, nor was my brother John, nor were
    any of my other sisters.
And that is why poor Dorothy had no one to point
    to!

ABOUT THE AUTHORS

Papy is a professional mathematician. He has been a nonpermanent member of the Institute for Advanced Study at Princeton, and is now full professor of algebra at the University of Brussels.

Frédérique Papy also holds a doctoral degree in mathematics, and has taught mathematics to students of all ages.

In the last ten years both Papy and Frédérique have worked very hard to modernize the teaching of mathematics. They have written many books on mathematics and the teaching of mathematics, which have been translated into several languages. They have also created a new method for the teaching of mathematics.

ABOUT THE ILLUSTRATOR

Susan Holding studied at Smith College and Adelphi University and has recently received her degree in art from the Traphagen School of Fashion, where she was awarded several prizes.

In her free time Mrs. Holding enjoys racing on both small sailboats and on larger ones in overnight and ocean races. In the winter she likes to ski.

A native New Yorker, Mrs. Holding presently lives with her son in Larchmont, New York.